FLORA IN FOCUS

TREES
AND THEIR SHAPES

SMITHMARK

© 1995 Holding B. van Dobbenburgh bv
All rights reserved. No part of this publication
may be reproduced, stored in a retrieval system,
or transmitted in any form or by any means,
electronic, mechanical, photocopying, recording
or otherwise, without the prior permission of
the copyright owner.

For this English language edition:
Todtri Productions Ltd., New York

This edition published in 1996 by SMITHMARK
Publishers, a division of U.S. Media Holdings,
Inc., 16 East 32nd Street, New York, NY 10016.

SMITHMARK books are available for bulk pur-
chase for sales promotion and premium use. For
details write or call the manager of special sales,
SMITHMARK Publishers, 16 East 32nd Street,
New York, NY 10016; (212) 532-6600.

Editions of this book will appear simultaneously
in France, Germany, Great Britain, Italy and
the Netherlands under auspices of Euredition bv,
Den Haag, Netherlands

Photographs:
PPWW Plant Pictures World Wide, Daan Smit
Text:
Nicky den Hartogh
Translation:
Tony Langham
Concept, design and editing:
Boris van Dobbenburgh
Typesetting:
Mark Dolk/Peter Verwey Grafische Produkties
Color separation:
Unifoto PTY LTD, Cape Town
Production:
Agora United Graphic Services bv, 's-Graveland
Printing and binding:
Egedsa, Sabadell, Spain

ISBN 0-8317-6124-5

INTRODUCTION

Amongst the rich variety of plants in the natural world, trees are the largest and most striking. They make their mark on landscapes with very different natural environments. Even the biggest metropolis seems arid and lifeless without trees, despite all the hustle and bustle of city life.

Trees provide shade, coolness, protection and a sense of being connected with nature, even if all you can see from the window on the fourth floor is a branch or the crown of a tree which reflects the changing seasons.

A tree could be described as a woody plant with an extensive root system and a woody stem which branches out a little way above the ground and grows to a height of at least sixteen feet. In fact, this does not really tell you anything.

Trees provide food, medicine, oxygen, timber, raw materials for all sorts of products and many other things. A tree is also a miracle of buds, leaves and flowers, the rustling of the branches, the changing colors in autumn, the fragrance of the blossom and the smell of rotting leaves and the gnarled shape of the trunk which eternalizes the passing years.

Trees help to determine the character of the landscape; conversely the climate and composition of the soil in the natural environment help to determine the character of the trees.

In order to survive, they constantly have to adapt to factors which are characteristic of the area where they grow: the strength of the wind, the temperature, the amount of sunlight and rainfall, the nutrition or lack of it in the soil where they are rooted. All these factors contribute to the inexhaustible variety of shapes, varying from the smallest dwarf varieties in high mountainous regions, to the mighty giants of the rainforests, and from the exuberant splendor of flowering deciduous trees to the introspective austerity of coniferous trees.

In coastal regions trees are swept into beautiful shapes by the wind, but in places where the wind is always very strong, the leaves dry out and eventually the trees die. Nevertheless, there are trees which have adapted to this, such as the divi-divi (Caesalpina coriaria) in the Antilles. The crown of this tree grows into a flat horizontal shape formed by the wind.

When a young tree in the thickly overgrown tropical rainforest sees an opportunity to shoot up in a small clearing under the unbroken green canopy, it initially puts all its energy into growing upwards to become as tall as possible in the shortest possible time; it is only when it reaches the light that the trunk becomes thicker and a broader crown develops. The leaves of very different varieties of trees which grow in the crown layer of the rainforest have adapted to the high level of humidity; they have a smooth surface and end in a tapering point so that large quantities of water are easily drained off. At a lower level of the forest there are cacao trees (Theobroma cacao) and numerous other trees which produce large, often brightly colored flowers which grow from the trunk, so that they are easily accessible to bats, which pollinate them.

Large trees, such as Ceiba, Koompassia, Tecona and Triplochiton have developed enormous plank roots above the ground which provide the trunk with the necessary support in the soft soil of the jungle. These supporting roots can be so large that they can be used as timber for wagon wheels or whole doors. The deciduous trees in temperate regions lose their leaves in autumn before the tree roots can no longer draw up water from the soil when the ground is frozen, so that the trees will not dry out. Evergreen conifers have reduced their foliage to needles or scales to limit evaporation; on the savannahs, trees and tree-shaped succulents lose their leaves in the dry season or survive by drawing on the supplies of water stored in the trunks, branches and leaves.

High up in the White Mountains of California, where the polar climate has an influence on the vegetation up on the plateau, the "bristlecone pine" (Pinus aristata var. longaeva) grows extremely slowly, over a period which can stretch over almost fifty centuries. The apparently lifeless trunks produce only an occasional branch sparsely covered with leaves, because the growth of these unbelievably old trees, the longest living life forms on earth, has often stagnated for long periods because of the rugged climatological conditions.

One of the strangest trees in the world grows in the dry African savannahs, the baobab or monkey bread tree (Adansonia digitata). It has a squat, thick trunk and the branches sprawl out in all directions, and are leafless for most of the year.

As in most cases of curious natural phenomena, there is no lack of explanations for the existence of such bizarre shapes of trees. For example, it is said that when the devil became caught up in the branches of this tree, he was so furious that he ripped the tree out of the ground and put it back upside down, so that henceforth the roots would have to serve as branches.

Every traveler who has visited the regions where the baobab grows is familiar with this tree, because it is as characteristic of the dry African landscape as the Leaning Tower is of Pisa.

It is not the case that the special methods of growth which trees have developed in the course of hundreds of thousands of years to adapt to the natural environment disappear as soon as they are introduced into new areas by man.

For example, the swamp cypress (Taxodium distichum) will form the same breathing roots as it has in its original marshy habitat when it grows in higher areas, even though it no longer needs them in this new environment.

The flora, and therefore the landscape, are constantly subject to change because of human intervention. As long as the necessary products for man's consumption were collected in the woods, and only small areas of ground were temporarily cleared for farming purposes, the ancient woodlands, which date back to primeval times, and in which countless plants, animals and other organisms were interdependent, were able to survive in their original state. However, as a result of the large-scale clearance of agricultural land, the extensive grazing of domestic animals and deforestation for timber, the landscape has changed dramatically. In Western Europe the majority of the primeval forests which once covered the land had been completely destroyed by the Middle Ages, resulting in cultivated landscapes or infertile, eroded wastelands.

While trees were cut down in one place, man started planting trees in other places, as protection against the wind and the sun, to provide firewood and timber, and as fruit trees. Many centuries before the birth of Christ, crops were taken from their original habitat to be grown and cultivated in other places. Initially these were mainly "useful" crops, such as nuts, dates and olives. Later they also included ornamental trees. Many trees have been cultivated for such a long time that it is no longer possible to determine where they originated, and it is difficult to imagine that they were ever absent from the landscape in areas where they have formed part of the vegetation for so long.

After the Middle Ages, explorers and arborists came back from America with stories of giant forest trees which were taller than they had ever seen in Europe: the three-hundred-foot-tall redwood (Sequoia sempervirens), the sitka spruce (Picea sitchensis), and the Douglas fir (Pseudotsuga menziesii). The sitka spruce and the Douglas fir have been introduced to Europe and are widespread, but they will never be as impressive as in the densely overgrown, virgin forests where they were found originally.

Since then, a large part of the wealth of nature all over the world has been destroyed. However, following the enormous efforts of conservationists and environmentalists, an understanding has grown of the great importance of trees, woods and all the related life forms, for the continued existence of the earth.

This has resulted in the fact that relics from primeval times which were threatened with extinction, the mighty giant redwood tree and redwood in North America and the cycas palm in South Africa, can still be admired in their natural environment, even though only a small number remain to bear witness to their former glory.

At last, admiration is growing for the people of the forests who succeessfully grow so many different crops on limited surface areas that they are able to approach the layers of the rainforest and restrict soil erosion and exhaustion to a minimum.

The beauty of trees and their shapes is not limited to areas where the forests have remained untouched, or where particularly old, thick or tall specimens have survived.

In a cultivated country such as the Netherlands, where there is virtually no nature in the strict sense of the word, the landscape is determined by trees, precisely because it is so flat, and osiers and pollard willows deserve to be protected and respected every bit as much as the tree-shaped aloes in Southern Africa.

FAGUS SILVATICA (germinated plants)
Heavier fruit, such as acorns and beech nuts, falls not far from the trunk, and generally germinates close to the parent tree, unless carried away by animals. Like other deciduous trees, beech trees are bicotyledenous plants; in the beech nut there is a seed with two large cotyledons which contain a great deal of reserve nutrients. When the nut has fallen out of its woody cup and has spent the winter lying on the ground, it starts to draw water from the soil and germinates. First, a small root bores down into the soil, and after a few weeks it forms lateral roots. Then the two broad cotyledons unfold. These are completely different in appearance from the first true beech leaves which develop at the next stage.

A shady Japanese wood where only occasional rays of sunlight manage to penetrate the dense canopy of leaves. On the green mossy forest floor there are some beautiful camellia flowers, which have fallen from the tree in their entirety, without first losing any petals. Many camellias, including the tea plant (Camellia sinensis), originate from China. One of the indigenous varieties in Japan is the beautifully flowering Camellia sasanqua.

The buds of these deciduous trees which lose their leaves swell up in spring, and after a mild winter sometimes very early on in the year. Not long afterwards the leaf scales retract and the delicate leaves, which were formed in the previous summer, start to unfold. On warm days the leaves develop so quickly that you can sometimes hear the buds open in the woods.
As soon as the leaves have unfolded, the sap rises in the trunk. The process of photosynthesis in which hydrogen, oxygen and carbon dioxide are converted into sugars and starches, starts even before the leaves have grown to their full size.
In order to function properly, they need a lot of light. This is why many trees, including many maple varieties, form a so-called leaf mosaic. The length of the leaf stems are adapted in such a way that every leaf finds itself an open space where it can profit best from the light.

ACER JAPONICUM
Leaf growth in the Japanese maple (Acer japonicum) only gets underway half-way through the spring. The modest purplish-red flowers appear on the branches at the same time that the leaves unfurl.

LAGERSTROEMIA INDICA
When all the leaves have fallen from this tree in autumn at the end of the flowering season, the attention is focused completely on the trunk and branches. ▶

JUNIPERUS PHOENICEA

Tortured and twisted by the rigors of nature, Juniperus phoenicea manages to survive to a great age on the infertile, stony hillsides in the coastal region of Cyprus.

CUPRESSUS SEMPERVIRENS

The trunk of an ancient cypress tree which looks as though it has been carved (Cupressus sempervirens) on the Greek island of Crete. With age and in the harsh climatological conditions in which these trees sometimes have to survive, they assume the most fantastic shapes.

QUERCUS SUBER

In an old cork oak (Quercus suber) like this one - which is indigenous in southern Europe and the Balkans - the gnarled branches covered with thick cork bark form a fantastic open crown. The leathery, silvery-grey leaves protect the tree against losing moisture in summer. In the autumn the cork oak bears acorns of which the lower half rests in a fringed cup.

PINUS NIGRA PALLASIANA

The straight and sturdy trunk of a black pine (Pinus nigra pallasiana), which grows right up to the crown, ends in a bushy crown of rings of branches and dark-green clumps of pine needles. Initially, the pine trees have a more conical shape, and the stepped rings of branches conceal most of the trunk. As they grow older, many varieties gradually shed more and more of the lower branches and slowly a more spreading canopy or spherical crown develops.

MISODENDRON

The crowns of trees provide shelter for countless forms of vegetation. Apart from epiphytes - tree dwellers which survive independently without harming the host - there are also parasites and semi-parasites, such as the Misodendron, which is found in Chile and Argentina. This plant is related to the mistletoe, and nestles in the crown of Nothofagus varieties, depriving the tree of some of the nutrients it needs.

PINUS HALEPENSIS

The aleppo pine (Pinus halepensis) has a characteristic curved trunk which grows at a slight angle, and a rounded crown. It has been planted on a large scale in Mediterranean coastal areas, because of its capacity to grow in sandy soil and resist the salty sea winds.

PINUS PINEA

The curiously flattened crown of the parasol pine or Italian stone pine spreads out above the open undergrowth. This is one of the most characteristic trees in the Mediterranean landscape. Apart from the special shape of the crown, the parasol pine also produces strikingly large cones. They are a broad oval, or almost round shape and contain large seeds with a sweet taste, known as pine nuts or "pignons."

NOTHOFAGUS DOMBEYI

The Nothofagus varieties - the "beech trees of the southern hemisphere" - comprise both stunted dwarf varieties and sturdy woodland trees which grow vertically to a considerable height. The fact that Nothofagus is indigenous in the southern hemisphere, both in South America and in Australia and Asia, although these continents are separated by the Pacific Ocean, is considered proof that a hundred million years ago, these continents formed a single huge land mass.

ENCEPHALARTHOS TRANSVENOSUS

The thirty-foot-tall trunk of Encephalarthos transvenosus, a South African palm fern, is crowned by leaves which stand up stiffly. Palm ferns, or cycas palms, have been called living fossils because they have survived so many millions of years. They are relics from a time when dinosaurs and giant reptiles still lived on earth.

ALSOPHILA AUSTRALIS

The delicately patterned giant leaves unite to form a kaleidoscopic mosaic in Alsophila australis, a tree fern with a beautifully marked trunk which can grow to a height of twenty feet.

EUCALYPTUS BENTHAMII

The pale branches and hazy, greyish-green foliage of Eucalyptus benthamii. Of all the trees which grow in Australia, three-quarters are Eucalyptus varieties. Many of these have silvery, almost round leaves when they are young - very different from the elongated, willow-like leaves of mature specimens.

FITZROYA CUPRESSIOIDES

The bark of the alerce (Fitzroya cupressioides) can be several inches thick. This giant tree from the forests of Chile and neighboring Patagonia in Argentina was traditionally used by the Indians to caulk their boats. The wood of the alerce is particularly hard.

NOTHOFAGUS DOMBEYI

A solitary skeleton of Nothofagus dombeyi, bleached by the sun, in the area of Chile affected by an eruption of the Villarica volcano. Chile is a highly volcanic country which also suffers severely from earthquakes as a result of the many eruptions.

When a volcano erupts, it is not only the destructive force of the glowing stream of lava which affects the landscape, but a great deal of damage can also be done by showers of ash. Vast areas are covered by a choking layer of ash, and even when it is only a quarter of an inch deep, all the vegetation dies off. Although whole civilizations have disappeared under streams of lava and showers of ash, volcanoes also have a positive influence on the landscape and culture; it is no coincidence that it is precisely the slopes of volcanic mountains that are often so densely populated. After a while, the volcanic deposits are eroded, leaving extremely fertile soil. In tropical areas the process of soil erosion can even take place very quickly. As in the case of forest fires, the pioneering plants start by dominating the landscape. In Chile, this pioneer-ing vegetation includes Gunnera and Pernettya mucronata, which can be found wherever the mighty streams of lava once flowed.

A RTOCARPUS HETEROPHYLLUS
Nangas, or jackfruit, the edible fruit of Artocarpus heterophyllus, weighs between twenty-two to fifty-five pounds. These trees are cultivated in Indonesia and Thailand, amongst other places. Artocarpus is a cauliflorous tree, which means that the flowers and fruit grow directly on the low branches and trunk. This special phenomenon is found particularly in trees which originally formed part of the tropical rainforest. In the gloom of the bottom level of the forest, where flowers can barely be seen amongst the foliage, large and brightly colored flowers on the trunks are very striking. Consequently they attract the attention of bats and other low-flying or creeping creatures which pollinate them. After the pollination, the fruit that develops is usually large, with seeds containing a great deal of reserve nutrients, so that they can survive the competition to find a spot in the overcrowded soil of the jungle floor.

F ICUS BENGHALENSIS
A fruiting branch of the banyan (Ficus benghalensis). The flowers and fruit of this fig tree, which belong to the same family as jackfruit, also often grows on the trunk or thick branches.

C ERCIS CANADENSIS
Cercis canadensis is a wonderful sight when the tightly packed bundles of flowers appear on the trunk. The "Redbud," as the tree is known in its own country because of its red buds, grows in the forests of the eastern United States. In the trees of the Northern Hemisphere, cauliflori is rare. ▶

E UPHORBIA BALSAMIFERA

D RACAENA DRACO

The dragon's tree (Dracaena draco) is also indigenous in Tenerife. The "dragon's blood," the red sap, is used in red lacquers and varnishes. The oldest and most impressive specimen has become a national monument on the Canary Islands, and is even shown on banknotes. The tale that, according to popular tradition, it is thousands of years old, is probably fantasy. As in the case of palms or tree ferns, there are no annular rings in the dragon's tree, and therefore it is difficult to determine the age of a tree, even if it is a dead specimen.

E UPHORBIA BALSAMIFERA

In semi-deserts and deserts, plants live by drawing up and retaining the scarce amounts of water available by means of all sorts of ingenious systems. These include some very strange plants known as succulents. The landscape is characterized by gigantic cacti, tree-shaped spurges (Euphorbia varieties) and aloes, rather than by "ordinary trees." Tenerife, one of the Canary Islands, a group of islands which belongs to Spain, is the home of a large diversity of plants which thrive in dry conditions. These include Euphorbia balsamifera, a tree-shaped or bushy succulent, which sheds its leaves in summer to limit evaporation.

MAGNOLIA X SOULANGEANA

When it is in full blossom, the spreading common magnolia (Magnolia x soulangeana) has pride of place. The softly-hued, tulip-shaped flowers stand straight up on the branches before the leaves are completely developed. When the calyx opens in good weather, countless stamens are revealed around the pronounced heart. In temperate regions the most beautiful blossoms appear in spring at the time of new growth. Trees which are particularly striking are those which depend on insects to be pollinated, such as cherry trees, apple trees and magnolias. The color, size and fragrance of the blossom is aimed at attracting insects which fly from tree to tree on their search for nectar and cross-pollinate them.

A ESCULUS X CARNEA "BRIOTII"

The deep red color of the upright candles is repeated in the main vein of the leaves which have already unfurled. Despite the wealth of flowers, the red horse-chestnut (Aesculus x carnea "Briotii") does not bear much fruit in the autumn.

P YRUS COMMUNIS

One of the many cultivated varieties of the common pear tree (Pyrus communis), which blossoms prolifically. Such an ordinary tree, and yet such a wonderful surprise every spring. The blossoms may serve primarily to produce a rich crop of fruit, but flowering fruit trees also attract countless admirers every year.

PRUNUS SERRULATA "SENRIKOH" (fallen petals)
There are numerous varieties of Japanese ornamental cherry trees. The color of the blossom varies from the predominant bright pink of the well-known Prunus serrulata "Kanzan" to the modest, pale-pink of Prunus serrulata "Senrikoh." Japanese garden and landscape architecture has attached so much importance to ornamental cherry trees for hundreds of years, that the search for even more beautiful forms and their cultivation has been refined to a true art. In spring, the Japanese flock to experience the effect of the breathtaking wealth of blossoms. The blossoming hills exert a wonderful charm because Prunus varieties have been selected with a natural shape and soft hues of the simple flowers. In Japan, the more striking ornamental cherries with double flowers are generally grown away from other trees.

FICUS ELASTICA

The foot of Ficus elastica, which originates in India and Southeast Asia, consists of an extensive network of snake-like roots. In several members of the Ficus family the root formation is so intriguing that the leafy part of the tree goes almost unnoticed. The banyan tree (Ficus benghalensis), which develops a gigantic structure of prop roots, is particularly well known.

KOOMPASSIA EXCELSA

Enormous prop roots strengthen the foot of Koompassia excelsa, which grows to a great height. This tree is the king of the jungle which covers a large part of the Indonesian island of Borneo. Many tropical tree varieties do not form a deep system of roots because the nutrients they need are in the top layer of humus on the jungle floor. The roots rarely go down further than three feet. Many different kinds of supporting roots above the ground serve to anchor the trunk securely, particularly when the tree is growing in soft, marshy ground. When the soil is deficient in oxygen in wet areas, for example, in the flooded forests where stilt trees and other mangroves deposit the silt, the roots above the ground also serve to supply oxygen.

COUSSAPOA DEALBATA

The immense system of prop roots of Coussapoa dealbata from Brazil serves as a trunk. As a young plant, Coussapoa grows as an epiphyte in the forks of a tree, living on the nutrients in the moisture and organic waste which have collected within reach of its roots. As it grows, more and more prop roots develop, slowly reaching down to the earth, and quite frequently choking its host.

CEIBA PENTANDRA

The kapok tree (Ceiba pentandra), which is extremely common in many tropical areas because of the kapok culture, grows to a height of 165 feet, and can have a diameter of six and a half feet above the supporting roots. Old trees are supported by enormous diagonal plank roots which can be as high as ten feet. The bark starts off green and later becomes grey and is covered with spines. The fruit of the tree are about six inches long and contain seeds embedded in woolly fiber, which was traditionally used as a material for insulation and stuffing, though it is becoming less and less common.

PANDANUS UTILIS

Pandanus utilis, the screw pine, puts down stilt-like prop roots to support the trunk. This tree is indigenous on the island of Madagascar.

CHORISIA SPECIOSA

In the floss silk tree (Chorisia speciosa) the bottom of the thorny trunk is much thicker than the rest.
The floss silk tree originates from Brazil and Argentina. The tree produces large fruits up to eight inches long, full of a soft, silky fluff, so that the seeds are dispersed by the wind over long distances. The local population use this fluff for stuffing cushions. The floss silk trees obviously have a tendency to become oversized, because the trunk of C. speciosa has the shape of a broad-bottomed bottle. The local people refer to these trees as "palos borrachos," i.e., drunken trees. They are found in dry forests and store moisture in the spongy wood for periods of drought.

TAXODIUM DISTICHUM

Although the marsh cypress (Taxodium distichum) originates in the marshes of the southeastern United States, it is also cultivated on higher, moisture-retaining ground, where it thrives. This specimen is in a botanical garden in Tokyo, and does not grow in or by the water, though it has still developed knee or breathing roots which look just like those of the trees found in the natural habitat.

TAXODIUM DISTICHUM

The seasons certainly do not go unnoticed for the marsh cypress. In autumn, this conifer puts on its golden finery; in spring, the branches are covered with fresh young greenery. Compared with many evergreen conifers, there are very few varieties which lose their foliage. Apart from the marsh cypress, metasequoia and larch are examples of this small minority of conifers which are bare in winter. The needles of Metasequoia glyptostroboides, the marsh cypress's closest relative, turn a beautiful coppery-brown color before they are shed. The larch has a magnificent golden-yellow autumn color, and in spring passers-by are spellbound by the delicate pale-green needles which form rosettes on the branches.

TAXODIUM DISTICHUM

In order to survive the flooding and hurricanes which are common in its natural environment, the swamp cypress has adapted to these conditions in an admirable way. It develops a deep and extensive root system under the ground, and from these roots grow strange wooden stumps which appear above the ground like little towers in a wide area around the trunk. These knees or breathing roots provide the tree with oxygen and also give support in the soft marshy ground. A structure of roots which broaden out towards the foot of the tree, also helps to anchor it more firmly.

SALIX X RUBENS

Osiers with Salix x Rubens, by a stream on the Portuguese island of Madeira. The young, still flexible willow shoots are used, amongst other things, for the wickerwork in chairs, and are harvested annually. Because of the enormous growth of the willow, the stumps regenerate without any difficulty after the osiers have been cut.

SALIX ALBA

In spring, the white willow (Salix alba) is covered in a haze of green foliage. The Netherlands provides a perfect habitat for the water-loving willow, and the pollard tree is a characteristic feature of the landscape. Now that these willows have lost their economic importance as a convenient source of timber for farmers, the maintenance is carried out by volunteer organizations (the branches have to be removed every three or four years) to prevent this special shape of tree from being lost.

EUCALYPTUS TORQUATA
As soon as the coral-red buds appear in groups between the silvery-grey foliage, the "coral gum" (Eucalyptus torquata) from Western Australia reveals its beautiful charm. It is only when the cover of initially stiffly closed cup-shaped flower buds is lost that the delicate red bunches of stamens appear.

AESCULUS X CARNEA
The upright candles of the red horse-chestnut (Aesculus x carnae) are four to six inches long and vary in color from red to a more pinky red. ▶

CRYPTOMERIA JAPONICA

An ancient, spreading Japanese cypress (Cryptomeria japonica) in the English county of Cornwall. There are many imaginative stories about the gigantic thickness of the trunk, the towering crowns, the great ages - in other words, the miraculous aspects of these champion trees. One Japanese cypress is said to have lived for more than seven thousand years. No specimen has ever been found which approaches anything like this age, so this story is most probably not based on fact, though the tree can undeniably live to an extremely old age. The redwood (Sequoia sempervirens) and giant redwood tree (Sequoiadendron giganteum), both indigenous in California, are among the world's oldest trees with an age of two to three thousand years, but they are both surpassed by the bristlecone pine (Pinus aristata var. longaeva). Research has shown that this slow-growing fir tree has survived in the White Mountains of California for almost five thousand years. Although reference is often made to oaks and ashes which are a thousand years old, European trees are rarely older than several centuries, and the taxus (Taxus baccata) and olive tree (Olea europaea), which sometimes grow more than a thousand years old, are amongst the oldest trees.

FRAXINUS EXCELSIOR

This squat ash (Fraxinus excelsior) in England is more than
two hundred and fifty years old; for a European tree this is a
very respectable age.

A DANSONIA DIGITATA

When the baobab or monkey bread tree (Adansonia digitata) loses its leaves during the long, dry season in the African savannah, it is able to survive because of the reserves of moisture stored during the rainy season in the spongy, grotesquely swollen trunk. The circumference of the trunk can grow to eighty-two feet, making this quite an impressively fat tree.

The Mexican cypress (Taxodium mucronatum) holds the world record for being the fattest tree. "El Giganti," a colossal specimen which has stood in the cemetery of Santa Maria del Tule in Oaxaca (Mexico) for at least fifteen centuries, has a circumference of more than 115 feet, measured at chest height, the usual way of determining the thickness of the trunk. However, it is arguable whether this claim is justified, because it is probable that the tree consists of several trunks which have grown together.

A DANSONIA DIGITATA
In the course of its long life - it is said that it can grow for thousands of years - the slow-growing baobab is extremely useful to its environment. Birds nest in its branches, children pick the leaves which are used to make soups and sauces, the fibrous bark is used for rope, old hollow trunks provide temporary accommodation and serve as a storage place for food and water. Large, fragrant flowers appear on the curiously-shaped branches of the baobab. These are pollinated by bats, and when they have been fertilized, they develop into sour-sweet fruit which are edible for man and animals.

OLEA EUROPAEA

The sun gives the leaves of the olive tree (Olea europea) a silvery shine, so that the broad spreading crown lights up. During his time in Provence (France), the painter Vincent van Gogh was struck by the constantly changing colors of the olive groves as much as by the dark, almost black color of the cypresses. Both characterize the picturesque landscape of Mediterranean regions.

CHAMEACYPARIS FUNEBRIS

Cypresses have been a source of inspiration to poets and painters for centuries. This cypress (Cupressus funebris) is a Chinese variety which was first brought to Europe in about 1850. In the Provencal landscape of southern France, where Van Gogh painted his black "flaming" cypresses during the last period of his life, the pillar-shaped Cupressus sempervirens is characteristic.

P LATANUS X ACERIFOLIA
These trees constantly change as the years pass by. In this ancient plane tree (Platanus x acerifolia), the once striking, spotted smooth bark is replaced by a more evenly colored rough bark.

A RBUTUS UNEDO
The flaking, gnarled trunk of the strawberry tree (Arbutus unedo), one of the few tree-shaped members of the heather family (Ericaceae) has a warm, reddish-brown color.

EUCALYPTUS GUNNII

Eucalyptus gunnii. The color and structure of the bark can be extremely characteristic of the many varieties of eucalyptus. The bark flakes off in long strips, or like pieces of a jigsaw, revealing the inner bark, and resulting in intriguing patterns of colors and shapes.

EUCALYPTUS DEGLUPTA

Eucalyptus deglupta sheds its bark in narrow strips. The outer part of the bark, known as cork bark, serves as a protective skin, enclosing the vital parts of the trunk where the sap rises from the roots to the crown and goes back down. The living layer of cells between the bark and the wood is protected against drying out, frost, sunburn, and the germs which cause diseases by a strong, watertight outer layer. Some trees have an evil-tasting, poisonous or spiny bark which protects them from being eaten by animals. The appearance of the bark is determined to a great extent by the particular variety, and helps to identify the tree. As regards its color, structure and thickness, there are great differences between individual trees, varying from the wafer- thin white bark of the birch to the reddish-brown, cork-like bark of the giant redwood tree which is one inch thick. The trunk can be armored so effectively that it is impossible for spores of fungi or other germs carrying disease to penetrate, so that the tree's vitality remains unaffected, even after a forest fire. When it grows old, the bark is usually characterized by a pattern of ridges and grooves, or overlapping plates which can become detached as the trunk increases in size. In several trees - Eucalyptus and Luma apiculata are striking examples - there is a continual process of renewal because older strips of bark are constantly shed at the surface.

CEIBA PENTANDRA

The poisonous spines on the green trunk of Ceiba pentandra, the kapok tree, effectively protect it against being eaten by animals.

CORNUS OFFICINALIS
Patterns of flames on the trunk and thick branches of a cornel (Cornus officinalis), which originates from Japan and Korea.

POPULUS NIGRA
A detail of the trunk of the poplar tree (Populus nigra), showing the deep grooves which are green with the growth of algae.

PINUS PINEA
For many pine trees the bark, which breaks up in irregular plates, is a characteristic feature of the trunk.

ACER GROSSERI
Several varieties of maple, including the Acer grosseri from China illustrated here, are eye-catching because of their beautifully striped bark.

CYTTARIA ON NOTHOFAGUS

Within the ecosystem of the forest, fungi fulfill an important function. They help to convert dead leaves and wood into organic particles which are beneficial to trees. The thin filaments of some fungi attach themselves to the roots of certain trees as "mycorrhiza" (fungal roots); the symbiotic exchange benefits both the fungus and the tree.

On the other hand, despite their sometimes fairytale appearance, tree fungi can be formidable parasites which survive at the expense of the living tree. By the time they produce fruiting bodies (which form the toadstool or fungus), so that they are visible to the eye, the concealed parts of the fungus have already done a great deal of damage in the trunk or roots of the tree. In the Nothofagus forests of South America, New Zealand and Australia, trees often succumb to Cyttaria, a trunk parasite which is found only on Nothofagus. The affected trees are covered in striking growths, often the size of a child's head, covered in tightly packed, white or yellowish round fruiting bodies. For the forest dwellers of Patagonia and Tierra del Fuego, who virtually died out after the arrival of the white man, these toadstools were an important source of food

PINUS RADIATA

Compared with deciduous trees, which constantly change their appearance with the recurring cycle of the seasons, evergreen conifers seem to lead a monotonous life. Nevertheless, all sorts of changes take place in these seemingly unchanging fir trees and majestic spruces. In spring the young shoots develop and yellowish-green, greyish-blue, yellow, red or purple inflorescences appear. The mantle of needles is constantly renewed, even though this happens so gradually that it cannot be observed with the naked eye.

The cones develop from female inflorescences. There are several varieties of pine trees in which the cones remain closed for a long time, sometimes as long as twenty years, waiting for conditions which are sufficiently favorable for the woody cone scales to open and release the seeds to the earth.

All trees in which the female infloresence develops into a cone are included amongst the conifers. They have needle-shaped or scaly leaves which, with only a few exceptions, remain on the branches in winter and therefore continue to provide nutrients throughout the year.

Conifers evolved a long time ago, long before deciduous trees, and they are past their greatest glory. Nevertheless, among the approximately 650 remaining varieties, there are many which are still unparalleled in strength, age, height and hardiness, such as the Douglas fir (Pseudotsuga menziesii), the giant fir (Abies grandis), the Japanese cypress (Cryptomeria japonica) and the giant redwood (Sequoiadendron giganteum).

The majority of conifers are found in the northern hemisphere; in the tropics they grow mainly in mountainous regions with a cooler climate. In contrast with the varied composition of tropical rainforests, the infinite pine forests of temperate zones contain only a few varieties. In the dense, dark forests they lose their lower branches because of the lack of light, and grow into absolutely vertical tall trees which are eminently suitable for the timber industry.

Conifers appear to be specially adapted to deal with difficult conditions. They are found in both wet and extremely dry soil, can root into permanently frozen soil, and are able to survive in infertile, sandy soil and loose , stony earth on mountain slopes. Taking into account the fact that conifers generally grow into very tall trees, there is a surprising number of small, spherical, cone-shaped and creeping conifers which are planted in gardens. Nevertheless, these dwarf varieties are direct descendants of their enormous ancestors. The seeds of certain conifers from time to time produce natural varieties which have a different shape or color from the parent tree. When these are discovered by nurserymen, they will try to propagate such varieties asexually, so that the special qualities are retained. Attractive garden conifers can also be cultivated from a different branch or top cuttings. Some dwarf varieties originate in high mountainous regions, where they adapted to the climatological conditions with a more stunted growth.

In the "Monterey pine" (Pinus radiata) the cones remain on the branches unopened for many years. This variety is indigenous in the United States, but is planted in many other countries as an ornamental tree and in reforestation projects.

CRYPTOMERIA JAPONICA
The vertical trunks of Cryptomeria japonica, the Japanese cypress, rise up above the granite altars of the centuries-old temple complex of Nikko (Honshu, Japan). In Japan, the sugi, as it is known there, is a sacred tree and is often planted by temples. The avenues planted with Cryptomeria in Nikko on Honshu in 1625 are particularly famous. Altogether they stretch out over a distance of sixty miles. Although they form an important attraction, there are many older Cryptomerias in other places in Japan. In the forests on the island of Yaku-shima, some specimens are believed to be almost 2,000 years old.

SEQUIOADENDRON GIGANTEUM
The giant redwood tree (Sequoiadendron giganteum), grows to a dizzying height in the favorable climate of California, and the trunk develops to a circumference which makes it the thickest tree in the world after Taxodium mucronatum. All the ancient giant redwoods in the United States are protected because they were threatened with extinction by lumberjacks. Now they attract large numbers of tourists. One of the oldest giants, known as "General Grant," is almost three hundred feet tall and the trunk has a diameter of approximately twenty feet. The crown of an old giant redwood tree, and that of its slenderer cousin, the redwood (Sequoia sempervirens) is as high as a skyscraper. The lower branches, which can develop up to a diameter of six feet, and are often compared to oak trees as regards size, stretch out one hundred feet above the ground. A thick cork bark protects the tree against diseases and forest fires.

PINUS BRUTIA

A witch's broom has formed on the branch of Pinus brutia. A fungus has affected the last bud on the twigs and dormant buds have developed here. The twigs have also been infected, and in their turn form lateral twigs until eventually a thick clump develops. This sort of mutation can be important for cultivators; many dwarf varieties of conifers were produced from such mutations in growth.

PINUS HALEPENSIS

The shape of the aleppo pine (Pinus halepensis) is outlined above the trees surrounding a villa near Nice (France).

ERYTHRINA CRISTA-GALLI (flowering branch)
Erythrina crista-galli, the coral tree, comes from Brazil. The rather inelegant tangle of thick thorny branches of the tree in its natural state draws the eye to the charming bunches of flowers. Apart from this tree, there are many other varieties of Erythrina with strikingly beautiful red flowers. Its scientific name refers to this color; the Greek word "erythros" means red. Several varieties are planted as ornamental trees in parks and gardens in countries with a tropical or sub-tropical climate. In its natural habitat the tree is pollinated by birds, the African varieties by honey birds, the American varieties by hummingbirds.

Erythrina crista-galli was first imported to Europe (Italy) from America in 1633. It was almost a hundred and fifty years before the tree was introduced to countries further north. In regions where it is too cold in winter for sub-tropical plants to survive, it is now one of the most popular plants grown in tubs, because the spectacular flowers of the coral bush are very attractive on roof gardens and verandas in the summer months. The plant is taken indoors for the winter and kept in cool but frost-free conditions, and can then go outside as soon as the danger of frost has passed. If is looked after carefully, Erythrina can reach such a great age, even in a tub, that it can become a family heirloom.

HEDERA HELIX

The forest floor is completely covered by ivy (Hedera helix) in a shady park in Wörlitz, Germany. The canopy of tree-tops allows very little light to penetrate, and the forest floor is determined for a large part of the year by the foliage of plants which prefer the shade, until bulbs and other spring flowers appear above the ground in spring, and the little flowers open as if by magic in the spring sunshine, before the leaves of the deciduous trees have fully developed.

FAGUS SYLVATICA

A velvety soft carpet of moss stretches out at the foot of the trunk of a large beech tree (Fagus sylvatica). Bushes and other plants usually have little chance of developing under the dense crown of the beech tree, because of the dark shadows and the effect of a compact system of roots close to the surface.

TILIA PLATYPHYLLOS

Some trees are inextricably linked with certain places and cultures, for example, the taxus "belongs" in a graveyard, the ginkgo in a Japanese temple, plane trees on a square, a pollard willow by a ditch, and lime trees (here Tilia platyphyllos) by a farmhouse.

BOUGAINVILLAEA
SPECTABILIS
Portugal: bougain-
villaea in full bloom.

MORUS NIGRA
A mulberry
tree (Morus nigra)
pruned into shape
on the island of
Crete. The trunks
are painted white to
repel insects.

BANKSIA SERRATA

The flowerheads and seed cones of Banksia serrata. Originally, Banksia was indigenous in the subtropical regions of Australia. In South Africa, Banksia serrata is cultivated specially for its large flowerheads. They are used in flower arrangements.

ALBIZIA JULIBRISSIN

Albizia julibrissin has plumy inflorescences above the saw-toothed leaves. Although its natural habitat is in Asia, this graceful little tree has become so common in European areas with a subtropical climate that it seems to belong there.

EUCALYPTUS FICIFOLIA ▶

A RAUCARIA ARAUCANA

Araucaria araucana, the Chile pine, also known as the monkey puzzle tree, grows in the middle of the plains of the Chilean landscape. The large seeds of this striking-looking conifer used to be a source of food for the Indians in this region. In 19th-century England the monkey puzzle tree became extremely popular not long after it was first introduced, and these bizarre and clearly imported trees can still be seen in many front gardens. The monkey puzzle tree has such peculiar branches that it is not comparable to any other tree. The branches are covered with tightly-packed reptilian scales, which become very tough and end in a sharp point.

A RAUCARIA ARAUCANA

NOTHOFAGUS DOMBEYI
Volcanic landscape in Chile. A few
cimens of Nothofagus dombeyi have sur
amongst the dead, white trunks.

ARAUCARIA ARAUCANA
The cactus-like plants are
young shoots at the foot of
Araucaria araucana, the monkey
puzzle tree. Even a well- developed trunk is initially completely
covered with pointed green scales,
and becomes bare only at a later
age.

AUSTROCEDRUS CHILENSIS
A forest of slender
Austrocedrus chilensis, a South
American member of the cypress
family.

ALOE PILLANSII

Aloe pillansii is rather like an extraterrestrial creature with the white tentacle-like rosettes of leaves at the end of its branches. By moonlight, the tree-shaped aloes have a ghostly effect on passers-by, particularly in places where there are several specimens together. In South Africa these curious succulents are protected.

POPULUS NIGRA

QUERCUS ROBUR
A fairytale tree on lion's feet, taking us back to a past when trees still had magical powers and the voices of the gods could be heard in the rustling branches. ▶

ANACARDIUM OCCIDENTALE

Anacardium occidentale is cultivated for its fruit in many regions with a tropical climate. The fruit contains edible seeds, so-called cashew nuts. The tree originates from the "dry forests" of tropical America and is particularly valuable because it is possible to reap a good harvest even in dry areas where few fruit trees flourish. Evaporation is reduced by the shiny, leathery leaves which restrict the loss of moisture to a minimum.

CASTANEA SATIVA

By the time the leaves have turned a golden autumn color, the shiny, brown, ripe nuts of the sweet-chestnut (Castanea sativa) pop out of their rough husks with their soft thorns. The sweet-chestnut tree is indigenous in Western Asia, North Africa and Southern Europe. In colder northern regions, where it is planted as an ornamental tree, the nuts do not always mature fully in the autumn.

EUPHORBIA COOPERII

Euphorbia cooperii grows in the South African provinces of Transvaal, Natal and Swaziland. The swollen pear-shaped segments forming the candelabra-shaped branches are characteristic. In southeast Africa the dry savannah is dominated here and there by magnificent tree-shaped Euphorbias. When there has been a lot of rain, a great deal of moisture collects in the succulent trunk and branches, and the plants are sustained by this during the dry season. Euphorbias are armed with spines to prevent them from being eaten by animals. In addition, they contain a poisonous sap. The sap of Euphorbia cooperii is so strong that contact with the skin causes irritation.

FAGUS SYLVATICA
Stately avenues of beech trees can be found in many regions in Europe. The trunks of the common beech (Fagus sylvatica) remains smooth for a long time, but when it grows old, the trunk has a muscled surface, as can be seen in this avenue of trees with pruned crowns.

QUERCUS ILEX

A wooded bank with holm oak (Quercus ilex) at Mawgan Helston, in the English county of Cornwall. As more and more forests, woodland and copses between fields disappear because of the urban sprawl and changing methods of agriculture, the importance of trees for planting by roads, streets and lanes increases. There are innumerable varieties. Every year nurseries produce new, cultivated varieties, even straighter, even more tapering, even more resistant to atmospheric pollution, varieties which thrive in the asphalt jungle requiring even less maintenance, and varieties which are wind and disease resistant. Nevertheless, there are still some wonderful winding country lanes with sloping banks on either side where ferns, wood violets, and solomon's seal find a place in the shade of the undergrowth.

P INUS PINEA
Pinus pinea, the parasol pine from the Mediterranean, is characterized by heavy, almost horizontal spreading branches.

L UMA APICULATA
Luma apiculata is indigenous in Chile and Argentina. This tree becomes more beautiful with the passing years. The branches and trunk have a striking golden, smooth bark, and rise up from the weathered root at the foot. Even a collapsing specimen, such as that shown in this photograph, continues to produce young shoots.

QUERCUS ROBUR

Quercus robur, the common oak, grows on its own away from other trees, as in the garden of Malahide Castle in Dublin. It has a short trunk, and the heavy main branches develop from fairly low down. In the past, an oak tree with curved branches was of incomparable value. The curved timber was carefully chosen and served as the timber in the shipbuilding industry to join the deck and the bilge.

Huge forest fires, which can hardly be contained, break out from time to time in Australia, southern Europe and the United States. They can result in unquestionable environmental disasters. Rare varieties of plants and animals are lost in the searing sea of flames, the bare wastes are left vulnerable to eroding forces, and the ecological balance can be disturbed for years, or even centuries.

These forest fires consume everything in their path, and the flames race from crown to crown with amazing speed, whipped up by strong winds. The so-called "crown fires" usually take place after a long period of drought.

A running fire, which does not burn much higher than the forest floor, the bushes and small trees, is easier to control. The inhabitants of forest areas have always been aware that the danger of forest fires can be turned by starting fires themselves on a limited scale. In this way, all the dead wood and leaves are cleared, creating bare areas which hold back the big forest fires. The North American Indians controlled the huge pine forests in this way, and the Australian aborigines used the same technique in eucalyptuss forests.
Trying to avoid all risks of fire, man started fighting fire in the natural world as soon as he had the means of doing so, but gradually it became clear that this was not always useful. Certain types of forest need fire to survive. In places where the natural course of events was frequently disrupted by fire fighters, a small number of varieties became dominant after a while, and valuable trees were doomed to extinction because they were unable to compete with these. Nowadays a method of controlled fire has been adopted, so that only the large forest fires are fought, and small fires are kept under control.
After the fire the forest usually regenerates itself because the trees germinate easily in the fertile earth of the clearings, and with an excellent sense of timing, the pioneers of the plant world take over.
Many trees have adapted to the fact that the fire breaks out at set times, e.g., as a result of lightning. The hard capsules of eucalyptus trees spring open forcefully in the fire and the seed is dispersed over a large area. The giant redwood tree and pine trees open up their cone scales in the heat to release the seeds; when the fire has cleared the dense undergrowth in the forest, the germinating plants are assured of a good future in the clearings where they get plenty of light.

PSEUDOBOMBAX ELLIPTICUM
Pseudobombax ellipticum is
indigenous from Mexico to
Guatemala. Its flowers grow on the
leafless branches. The flowers con-
sist mainly of the shiny stamens,
which are more than five inches
long. In English-speaking countries
the Pseudobombax is sometimes
called the shaving-brush tree.

SONNERATIA GRIFFITHII

Trees which succeed in becoming established in coastal marshes flooded with seawater by means of ingenious adaptations, are called mangroves. They form the flood forests in tropical regions, sometimes rooting deep down in the salt water into sand and silt, poor in oxygen. Some mangroves have prop roots, with which they absorb oxygen from the air; others develop breathing roots, which rise up above the surface of the water like snorkels. The harmful salt is removed or stored in the inactive tissue of the tree. Mangroves anchor the mud brought in by the water, and protect the coast against erosion and whirlwinds.

Linnaeus classified palm trees in the order "principes," which means monarchs. They have a special place among trees. The trunks usually grow up vertically, and there are no branches anywhere. There is no layer of cambium, which produces the new layer of wood every year. The "wood" consists of a collection of tightly compressed, hard fibers. Palm leaves, the symbol of victory and triumph appear from the heart of the palm at the end of the trunk. Depending on the shape of the leaves, the plants are subdivided into fan palms and feather palms.

At first, the leaf is in one piece, but as it develops, it splits open along the folds, producing long leaf sections tapering to a point. The bases of the old leaves can often be seen underneath the crown, and in some palm trees the leaf bases join together to form a smooth crown stem which can have a striking color, as in the lacquer or lipstick palm. The majority of palms have the straight, proud trunk to which they owe their majestic name, but some members of the family have several trunks, or do not have any trunk or only a short one, while the creeper-like thorny stems of rotan palms (Calamus) can grow to a length of 164 feet. Palms supply a large number of products, including dates, coconuts, plalm oil and palm wine. the heart of some varieties is a particular delicacy. The sugar palm (Arenga pinnata) has inflorescences which are tapped for their sweet sap, from which sugar can be crystallized when it is boiled.

ARECA CATECHU

The nuts of the betel palm (Areca catechu) are the main component in so-called Shiriprium, a masticatory which has a slightly stimulating effect. Chewing betel leaves is a traditional custom, which is still common in large parts of southeast Asia. The betel palm is indigenous in the humid regions of tropical Asia, and was introduced into other warm countries throughout the word.

PHOENIX CANARIENSIS

The majestic Canary Island date palm (Phoenix canariensis) originally grew only in the Canary Islands, but from the end of the 19th-century it was planted as an ornamental tree in southern Europe, and has now become so widespread that it is an important factor in determining the appearance of towns.

CYRTOSTACHYS RENDA

The colorful lipstick or lacquer palm (Cyrtostachys renda) from Borneo, Malaysia, Sumatra and Thailand, is one of several palm trees which have more than one trunk. It owes its name to the bright red overlapping stems of the leaves. When the palm has reached its full height, - the bamboo-like trunks can grow from sixteen to thirty feet tall - the leaf bases form a striking colored stem at the bottom of the crown.

WASHINGTONIA FILIFERA

Washingtonia filifera, the desert fan palm or petticoat palm, from the north of California and Arizona in the United States, has a fibrous skirt of old dried-up leaves.

ARENGA PINNATA

A bouquet of palm fruit of Arenga pinnata, the sugar palm. ▶

Nowhere on earth is the plant world so varied as in the tropical rainforest. The trees are predominant, but ferns, mosses, fungi and herbs have just as important a share in this particular ecosystem. Every spot is used, and the layers of vegetation are striking. Often a distinction can be made between four or five separate layers in the rainforest. Bromelias and orchids grow in the forks of the trees, ferns in the crown layer drip with moisture, and crusty mosses hanging in long beards create a mysterious ghost-like atmosphere.

INDEX